Performers in Uniform
THE GOLDEN KNIGHTS

By Peter B. Mohn

Photographs courtesy of the
U.S. Army

 CHILDRENS PRESS, CHICAGO

Acknowledgments:

   Thanks to Glen Horn for the photos, and to Larry Hook for his technical assistance.
   And to the Black team of 1976, including John Corathers, Tom Delaney, Guy Leverett, Mike Bachan, Roger Dupuis, Tim McNeeley, Joe Moore, Al Dillon, Marty Martinez, Bill Wilson, and especially Team Leader Al Richardson.

Library of Congress Cataloging in Publication Data
Mohn, Peter B
   The Golden Knights.
   (Performers in uniform)
   Includes index.
   SUMMARY: Introduces the Golden Knights, the United States Army's parachute team.
   1. United States—Army—Parachute troops—Juvenile literature. 2. Parachuting—Juvenile literature. 3. Skydiving—Juvenile literature. [1. United States. Army—Parachute troops. 2. Parachuting. 3. Skydiving] I. United States. Army. II. Title.
UD483.M63   356′ .166′ 0973   77-6768
ISBN 0-516-01952-X

ON WITH THE SHOW!

From 12,000 feet, the airport looked like a postage stamp. Sergeant First Class Al Richardson peered out the open door of the roaring aircraft. He watched as two, bright yellow Xs appeared at each end of the main runway.

"Golden Knights air, this is Golden Knights ground," the radio crackled. "The Red Devils are off."

"Roger," Richardson answered. He motioned to Sergeant First Class Guy Leverett, who unsnapped his seat belt and stood up. Leverett would make the "flag jump" to open the air show.

The Red Devils, three tiny aircraft, climbed into the sky. About 20,000 people on the ground watched.

"Coming overhead now is the Golden Knights' Caribou," announced Bill Bordeleau, the master of ceremonies for the air show.

All eyes were on the sky now. People shaded their eyes from the hot sun. "We should see the jumper's smoke any moment now," Bordeleau announced.

In the aircraft, Leverett watched Richardson, who watched the ground. On the flight deck, the pilot, Dave Murphy, flicked a switch that lit a green light by the ramp. Richardson saw it and motioned. Leverett took two steps down the ramp. His third step took him into thin air.

In a split second, Leverett yanked a leather thong. It was attached to the trigger of a smoke flare attached to his heel. The flare lit and began to pour red smoke. Leverett pitched over into a belly-down, free-fall toward the earth.

Quickly, Leverett's speed built up to 120-miles-per hour—straight down. The wind tore at his gold jump suit, his helmet, and goggles. His arms and legs were spread. His knees bent. By changing the position of his hands, he could turn. He looked down at the airfield, then at a stopwatch on his chest. He had started the watch at the moment he jumped.

"Watch the jumper's smoke," Bordeleau told the crowd. "He will free fall for about another 30 seconds, then open his parachute. When his chute opens, the Red Devils will begin to circle him." The Red Devils (Pilots Charlie Hillard, Gene Soucy, and Tom Poberezny) had broken their tight formation. They were flying in toward the airfield.

Leverett watched his stopwatch. He was still in his belly-first, free-fall position. The watch ticked closer to sixty seconds. At sixty-five seconds, the smoke flare on Leverett's heel gave out. He shifted his arms and legs. Now he was falling feet-first. With his right hand, Leverett pulled his rip cord.

A small, black and white parachute sprang from the pack on his back. It pulled two slender nylon lines, attached to the main parachute. The main chute flew out and opened with a flutter. Leverett lit a second smoke flare on his heel and began to steer his parachute in a slow spiral.

About 500 feet above ground, Leverett reached up along his harness and found a thin white cord. He pulled it, and an American flag tied to the harness opened.

Using his steering lines, Leverett flew his parachute into its final approach. Lower and closer he came to the target, a short distance from the crowd.

When only a few feet from the ground, Leverett pulled down on his steering lines. His parachute "flared," or lost its lift. He touched down, taking two steps. Swiftly he turned to face his chute, which was dropping to the ground behind him. Sergeant Martinez caught the flag and kept it from touching the ground.

"And there he is," said Bordeleau, "Sergeant Guy Leverett of the Army Golden Knights in the flag jump." Leverett turned to face the people. He smiled and waved as the people applauded.

High above, the Caribou droned on through the sky.

In the back of the plane, the Golden Knights waited. The Caribou's engines were noisy. Most of the men wore ear protectors and talked with sign language. The Knights would make their first jump the minute the Red Devils landed.

On the ground, Leverett (the flag jumper), Bordeleau (the announcer), and Martinez (the ground support man) watched the Red Devils. When the three, small aircraft were ready to land, Leverett picked up his walkie-talkie.

"Golden Knights air, this is Golden Knights ground," he said. "The Red Devils are landing. You'll be on in five minutes or less." In the airplane, both Murphy, the pilot, and Richardson, the leader of the jump run, heard him.

"Golden Knights ground, Golden Knights air," Richardson said. "Roger. We're turning right now on our first jump run, over."

"Roger," said Leverett.

Sergeant Martinez moved down the flight line so the smoke from his flares wouldn't blow into the crowd. Bordeleau introduced Leverett. Then the tall, slim sergeant took the microphone.

"If you will look overhead," he said, "you will see the aircraft. It is flying at 12,000 feet, the right altitude for a jump. In a minute, the first two jumpers will be away."

The ramp of the Caribou opened for the second time. Richardson again stood by the open door and watched the ground. Sergeants William Wilson and John Corathers unsnapped their seat belts, stood, and walked toward the ramp. Corathers carried a 14-inch mahogany baton.

"Our first jump this afternoon will be the baton pass,"
Leverett told the crowd. "In a moment, two jumpers will
come out of the aircraft. While in their 120-mile-an-hour,
free-fall, one of them will pass a special baton to the other."
Suddenly two smoke trails appeared behind and below the
Caribou. "The jumpers are out!" Leverett cried.

Jumpers Wilson and Corathers fell quickly. Both were in a free-fall position, about six feet apart. Both lit their smoke flares. They were so high only their smoke was visible from the ground.

Slowly and carefully, the jumpers "flew" toward one another. Corathers still held the baton tightly in his hand. They came within reach. Wilson grabbed the baton and Corathers let go. They flew apart again and continued to fall. Sixty seconds after they jumped, Wilson and Corathers turned away from each other. Both pulled their ripcords, and moments later, their parachutes opened.

The crowd sighed with relief as the two black and gold chutes opened. As soon as the men were on canopy, Martinez threw a smoke flare. The white smoke showed the jumpers which way the wind was blowing.

Using their steering lines, Corathers and Wilson swooped and spiraled through the sky. Corathers was first to land on target. As his feet touched down, he turned to face his parachute. Quickly, he got his gear out of Wilson's way. Wilson also made an on-target, "stand-up" landing.

High above, the Caribou had flown almost a full circle. As it neared the drop point, Sergeant Tim McNeeley was waiting to jump.

"Our next jump, ladies and gentlemen, is one of our most thrilling," Leverett told the crowd. "We call it the cutaway. In this jump, a single jumper leaves the airplane. He deploys a parachute after his free fall. Then, by hauling down on the risers, he streamers his chute."

A "streamer" is a parachute that doesn't work.

"This may look and sound dangerous but it isn't" Leverett said. "Each member of the Golden Knights practices this jump. We have done it thousands of times. Look! The jumper is out."

Sergeant McNeeley had lit his smoke flares. He wore three parachutes. His main chute was on his back. His reserve chute was on his chest. The third parachute was just above the reserve. He counted as he fell, then pulled the ripcord of his third parachute. It opened with a "whack!" He drifted under it for several seconds. Then he reached up and pulled down hard on one side of the chute. Instantly, it turned into a useless, flapping hunk of cloth.

"The parachute has been streamered," Leverett announced. "The jumper will now cut it away."

In mid-air McNeeley calmly unsnapped the clips that held his streamered parachute to his harness. Using his hands in free-fall, he steered himself away from the dead chute. Then he pulled the ripcord for his main parachute.

"There we have the cutaway jump," Leverett said. Again, the crowd seemed relieved to see McNeeley make a stand-up landing just off the target. His streamered parachute landed long before he did.

Once again, the Caribou appeared overhead.

"On our next jump, two Golden Knights will show you how they can fly," Leverett said. "They will come out of the aircraft together. While in free-fall, they will separate as far as they can. Then they'll come back together. Sometimes the jumpers get a mile and a half apart. If the wind doesn't blow their smoke around, you will see them trace a diamond in the sky.

Sergeants Mike Bachan and Roger Dupuis jumped. Their red smoke flares burning, the men fell together for a few seconds, then turned. Quickly, their speed built to 120 miles per hour. They flew apart for almost 20 seconds, then turned and sped back towards one another. About 20 seconds later, their paths crossed. Behind and above them, a neat diamond was etched in red smoke across the sky.

Mike Bachan's parachute bloomed into a square canopy. But something went wrong with Roger Dupuis's chute. He had a streamer on his main parachute! He looked up. He saw some lines fouled around his parachute. Quickly, as Sergeant McNeeley had done before him, Dupuis unsnapped his parachute from its harness.

"I see we have had a malfunction with one of the
jumpers," Leverett told the gasping crowd. "Right now,
the jumper is cutting his main chute away, and in a moment
his reserve will open," Leverett said calmly.

"We probably won't see an on-target landing from this
jumper," Leverett added as the jumper's reserve chute
opened. "The reserves we carry are not as maneuverable as
our main chutes."

"The man is on the ground and he's okay," Leverett later
announced. "If you will look up again, you will see the
Caribou with our last four jumpers of the day.

"For our last jump, Sergeant Al Richardson will lead three other men in a formation flight. This is the same kind of formation the Blue Angels use. The only difference is these men use their bodies, not airplanes. Watch their smoke."

Four smoke trails close together showed the Golden Knights were in formation. Richardson was at the head. Sergeant Tom Delaney flew on his right "wing" and Sergeant Al Dillon was on his left. Sergeant Joe Moore flew in the "slot," behind Richardson and between the wingmen. They fell and flew in formation for almost 40 seconds, then separated. Each opened his parachute.

When Richardson, the last to land, had gathered his gear, the nine Golden Knights formed a line away from the platform. At a signal from Richardson, they double-timed over and stood at attention. Leverett introduced each man and gave his home town. He also told the crowd how many jumps each man had made.

"And now, here's our Golden Knights Caribou in its fly-by," said Leverett as the large plane buzzed the runway.

"The only part of our program that's left is to pack our parachutes," Leverett said. "We'll be doing that in just a few minutes. If any of you want help, we'll be glad to let you." He grinned.

"And now, may I leave you with this final thought. May all your days be prosperous, and all your Knights Golden."

PACKING UP

Announcer Bill Bordeleau caught Sergeant Richardson before he went to pack his chute.

"Al, it looks like we're going to have time at the end of the show," he said. "Want to jump again?"

"Sure," Richardson smiled. "What do you want? A star?"

"Sounds good to me," Bordeleau replied.

"You have it," Richardson said. He hurried off to tell the rest of the Golden Knights. They were in the middle of the crowd packing their parachutes.

A youngster followed Richardson through the crowd. He stood by as Richardson dropped his chute on the ground.

"Hey, you want to help me pack up?" Richardson asked the boy, Ronnie. He did. "Okay, sit down right here," said Richardson, spreading the parachute pack on the ground. He pulled the shroud lines tight and spread the canopy out.

"Aren't you afraid that your parachute won't open?" Ronnie asked.

Sergeant Richardson looked up and grinned. "We carry a reserve with us. If the first chute doesn't work, we have that," he answered.

"What if the reserve doesn't work either?"

"You have to believe it will," Richardson said. "You know what they say, don't you? It isn't the fall that kills you. It's the sudden stop at the bottom that hurts."

"How fast do you fall?" Ronnie asked.

"In free fall, about 120 miles an hour," Richardson answered. "After the chute opens, the rate is only about 14 feet per second."

"Isn't it scary to free fall?" asked Ronnie.

Richardson looked up and said, "It's fun."

"Well, didn't it frighten you at first?"

"No." Richardson stopped working on his parachute for a moment. "They have a system, you see? They start by getting you into shape. They teach you how to fall. Then they teach you how to jump. You get so used to the idea of jumping you don't even think about it."

Richardson went back to work on his parachute. He folded the black and gold canopy loosely. When it was folded, he picked it up.

"You can get up, now," Richardson told Ronnie. He put the canopy inside the pack and began to fasten it.

Other Golden Knights around the field were doing the same thing. When they finished packing, they slung their parachutes over their shoulders and headed back for the Caribou.

UNWINDING

The air show ended. For the second time that afternoon, the Golden Knights had jumped. They had repacked their parachutes and stowed them away in the Caribou. Then they got in their cars and headed for town.

At the motel Sergeant Richardson took two briefcases from his car and found his room. Once inside, he took off his gold-colored jumpsuit and shiny black boots. Leverett came in a few minutes later and did the same. Soon, other members of the team came in and sat down.

"Are we all here?" Richardson asked. Opening a briefcase, he pulled out a file folder. "Who counted the crowd today?"

"I'd say twenty thousand," said one of the Knights.

"More than that," said a second. "I'd say thirty."

"Any other guesses?" Richardson asked. There were none. "Okay. One says twenty and one says thirty. I'll say twenty-five thousand." He wrote the figure onto a form inside the folder. At the bottom of the form was a diagram. Richardson marked his landing points on the diagram and passed the form on. Each member marked his landing as well, then returned the form to Richardson. He put it back in his briefcase and pulled out a slip of paper.

"There's a parade tonight," he said. "We have to send one guy to ride on a float. Who wants to volunteer?" No one spoke.

"Aw, come on," Richardson said. Still no one spoke.

"Okay," said the leader. "Tom, you'll ride in the parade. Al and Mike, you'll go with me down to the American Legion meeting. Tomorrow morning at nine, Tim, Guy and John will meet with the Cub Scouts at the airfield while the rest of us go to the hospital. Okay?"

"What's ahead?" asked one of the Knights.

Richardson said, "Show tomorrow, some appearances Monday, then we take off for Pennsylvania on Tuesday."

"How soon do we get back to Fort Bragg?" another Knight asked. "Twelve days," Richardson answered. "This will be the longest trip of this season."

"As long as you guys are still here, let's talk about the chute malfunctions," Richardson said.

"I think it's the reefing line," said Roger Dupuis. "When I picked up my chute, the reefing line was fouled around the rest of the rigging."

"Are you packing your chute any differently?" Richardson asked.

"Not that I know of," Dupuis answered.

Richardson shrugged his shoulders. "Let's hope for better luck from now on," he said. "We can't keep going on like this. Take care, you guys."

One by one, the Golden Knights drifted out of the room.

JUMP SCHOOL

"It takes a special kind of man to be a paratrooper," said a Golden Knight. "First, you have to be willing to train. All paratroopers have to go through basic training (eight weeks) and infantry school (four weeks). Then you can go to jump school at Fort Benning, Georgia. That's four more weeks."

"At jump school, the first thing they do is make sure you're in shape," a Golden Knight explained. "That first part of jump school almost killed me," he continued. "It was almost nothing but P.T. (physical training). We trained all day. It was running, then calisthenics, then running. I ate like a horse, but didn't gain an ounce.

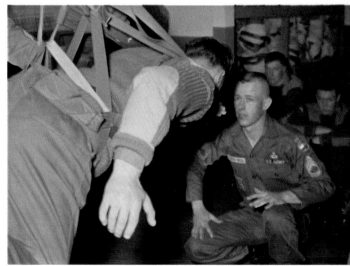

"Then you learn how to fall. It's a four-point fall—first your feet, then your lower legs, hips and upper body. Once you learn to do it right, you really shouldn't get hurt when you land.

"After that, it's learning how to jump, and you have to do *that* right too," he went on. "The only way they'll let you go out of the aircraft is with both hands on the sides of the reserve parachute, legs rigid, and your head down.

"In jump school, they have mock-ups of the aircraft. You jump out of them in a harness. One of your instructors sits right out in front and grades you. Until you do it right several times, they won't let you go out of a real aircraft."

The new paratroopers practice landing by sliding down cables. They practice jumping from towers. There, they buckle on harnesses attached to parachutes. Parachute and paratrooper are hoisted off the ground. When they reach to top of the tower, they are cut loose and float to the ground.

"We may make one or two tower jumps," a Golden Knight says, "before we go to the aircraft. By then, falling has become a way of life to us."

For the first jumps and many more after that, the chutes are packed by regular parachute riggers. "There is little or no fear that they won't open," a Golden Knight said.

Once a paratrooper has completed jump school and earned his maroon beret, his training doesn't stop. His jumping, at that point, is limited to "static line" jumps.

"A static line is attached both to the plane and the ripcord." says a team member. "When you're about ready to jump, the jumpmaster signals you to stand and to hook the static line to a cable over your head.

"Then, one by one, we jump when the jumpmaster tells us. The static line jerks the chute pack open and the canopy deploys. Then, all we have to worry about is the landing."

Paratroopers can go on to learn how to jump with specific weapons. Some may join the Special Forces, or "Green Berets." Others may go to what the Airborne calls "HALO" (High altitude, low opening) school to learn to free-fall.

"The whole idea behind HALO jumping is to be able to jump from a flying plane so high no one can see or hear it," explains a Golden Knight. "We may jump so high that we have to wear oxygen masks. But we won't open our chutes until we're down low."

Airborne personnel can carry up to 90 pounds of equipment with them when they jump. "We have special bags which we can lower. So the gear hits the ground a second or so before we do," a man explains. "The bag carries anything from weapons to food or medical supplies."

MAKING OF A GOLDEN KNIGHT

Each fall, notices are sent around the Airborne divisions. Any paratrooper with more than 200 jumps may volunteer for the Golden Knights. Each year about 200 men report to Fort Bragg, North Carolina, the home of the Golden Knights. From them, no more that 15 to 20 will be chosen for the three-year hitch with the team.

"We put the volunteers through the same routine we have the year long," Sergeant Glen Horn said. "They eat with us, train with us, and jump with us. Some of them decide rather early that this is too much, and go home. Our life isn't the easiest.

Every member of the team must be able to "do it all," Horn added. "A man can jump in one show, be ground support in the next, and narrate the next one," he said. "He has to be able to talk as well as make good jumps. And he must be dependable."

After several weeks of competing for a position in the
Golden Knights, the hard training ends. "By then, we know
all the guys," says a Golden Knight. "The team members
sit down and talk about each one. They choose the new men
and let them know. Those who weren't selected go back to
their old units.

"Not being chosen is no bad thing. The guys who don't
make it can be proud that they've tried. Some come back and
make it the second time. We like men who don't give up."

Late each year, the Golden Knights hold a reunion.
Each of the more than 150 members over the years is
invited. At reunion time, the new team members are
introduced. Those who are leaving the team are honored.

Many of the reunion events are held in the Golden
Knights' dayroom. Its walls are covered with mementoes of
their performances. The mementoes cover far more than
the Knights' jumps in the United States.

"Almost every parachute team in the free world has
come to train with us," Horn said. "We've gone to other
countries, too." He pointed to pennants given to the
Knights by groups from Europe, Asia, and South America.
Photographs of the United States and foreign jump teams
hang on the walls.

"These discs you see," he said, pointing to hundreds of
colored circles tacked to the arches of the dayroom, "are the
'dead-center' marks earned by our competition jumpers.
Any time a man gets a dead center in competition, they give
him the target. There are so many here, I've never tried to
count them."

"Reunion is a special time." Sergeant Richardson added. "We take this time to honor the Golden Knights of the past. And we make some people honorary Golden Knights."

"Tiny Broadwick is an honorary Golden Knight," Richardson said. "Tiny Broadwich was a well-known barnstormer years ago. A very small woman, she made many parachute jumps across the United States. Like Tiny Broadwick, most honorary Golden Knights have contributed to sport parachuting.

PRACTICE MAKES BETTER

The Army Golden Knights have been giving shows since 1959. The first parachute team had only a few people. By 1976, the Golden Knights numbered 62 and they had their first woman member. She was not a jumper, however.

"Now there are three Golden Knight teams," Sergeant Glen Horn explained. "There are two demonstration teams, the Gold and the Black. Then we have our competition team. Its members work on accuracy in landings and control in the air. That's a whole different thing."

A Golden Knight's day at Fort Bragg begins early with a four-mile run. Sometimes the men will run as a group. Other times, they run by themselves. At exactly 7:45 in the morning, they form outside their headquarters building for calisthenics and inspection.

When the physical training is completed, the Golden Knights go to their specific jobs, if they have them. Before that, however, their First Sergeant may have words for one or more of them.

"The First Sergeant is boss," says a Golden Knight.

"We all have different jobs," explains the operations officer for the Golden Knights. "I work on the team's show schedule for the year. One man is in charge of our parachute loft. He supervises the packing of reserve chutes and repairing of damaged ones.

"Others on the team are medics, supply people, flight crew, and clerks. We have an information specialist and a photographer with the team. Every person who wears a Golden Knights uniform came from an Airborne division, however."

On a jump day the team takes a bus to their jump zone. Even though Fort Bragg is the largest Army base in the United States, the Golden Knights have their own jump area 40 miles away.

"We have to have our own drop zone," Sergeant Bachan explained. "If we had to wait for normal airplane movements at a regular field, we couldn't jump as much."

A "Huey" helicopter waits at the jump site. Seventeen men have come out to jump. Some are members of the competition team. Others are part of the Black demonstration team.

The teammates pulled their gear from the bus. Two of them spread canvas on the field. It formed a cross—the jumpers' target. Two more hang up a black and gold wind sock. It would show the jumper which way and how hard the wind was blowing.

Sergeant Richardson called off nine names. "You will go on the first lift," he told them. "The guys from the Black team will go with me," Richardson said. "We're going to do some formation flying today."

Soon the Huey lifted off.

"How high can the Huey go today?" someone asked.

"The pilot said he could make ten to ten-five (thousand feet) with no trouble," Richardson said. The Huey flew away and began to climb. When it reached about 2,000 feet, two long streamers fell away from it.

Richardson watched the streamers fall almost straight down. "Good," he said. "Almost no wind. We'll have easy landings today." He picked up a "walkie-talkie."

"Golden Knights air, this is Golden Knights ground," he said. "How soon will the first men be out? Over." He listened. "Roger," he replied.

"They're passing through ninety-five hundred," he reported. "The next time around, they'll be hot. "Hot" means a jump run. He looked again at the sky.

"They're out," he said. Other strained to see the free-falling parachutists. Suddenly a black and gold canopy appeared in the sky. Soon, three more opened. A lone jumper came out of the helicopter next and drifted to the ground. Then four more men jumped.

Soon after they landed, the chopper zoomed in and picked up the other eight men. Within a few minutes, their parachutes were blooming black and gold against the blue Carolina sky. After the fourth lift, the helicopter returned to Fort Bragg for more fuel. The Golden Knights settled back in the shade to rest.

One of the jumpers began to fold his bundled-up parachute. "I think I'm going to like this after all," he said pointing to the chute. The Golden Knights switched in 1975 and 1976 to a square, "Strato-Cloud" parachute.

"You should," replied another. "Can you think of an easier-opening, softer-landing chute than this one?"

"We jumped a round parachute for years," Sergeant Joe Moore later explained. "It was called the Para-Commander. It wasn't a bad chute, but it did open hard."

The men heard the returning helicopter long before it appeared over the trees. By the time it landed on the grass, Richardson's group was ready for their formation jump.

"Hey, that was a good formation," said Richardson when he landed. "How long do you think we had it?"

"Forty-five seconds, maybe," replied one of his wingmen. "That is, if the slot got into position as quickly as everyone else."

"I was there, I was there," grumbled the slotman. In the formation, the wingmen are beside, but slightly behind the leader. The "slot" position is behind the leader and between the wingmen.

"How did the break look?" Richardson asked one of the men who had watched from the ground.

"Good. If you'd had smoke, it would have been a starburst," the man replied. To save money, the Golden Knights don't use smoke flares in their practice jumps.

"Sounds good," Richardson said. "I was afraid we were getting a little sloppy on that." He grinned. "Next lift, we're going to do a star. But don't tell anyone, okay? He looked up at a bunch of grins. Almost all sport parachutists enjoy doing stars.

In a star, the jumpers form a circle as they fall. Each jumper holds onto the hand or wrist of the jumper next to him. It takes skill to form one.

"It takes a lot of control to get into a star," Richardson explained. "The jumper can't move in too fast or heads bump. If he comes in too slowly, we might not have time to form it. We start with two, then three, four, five—however many jumpers we have. It's fun to do when we do it right."

Richardson and his group jogged out to the helicopter. Soon, their "bird" climbed through five thousand feet. With hand signals, Richardson told the flight crew he wanted 12,000 feet. He began to watch the ground.

Within minutes, the helicopter crossed over the field on a "hot" run. Richardson looked around at his teammates and grinned. Then he slipped out of the chopper and began a feet-first fall. In a couple of seconds, he pitched over into

the belly-first free fall position. He looked around. Slowly
and steadily, he cound see Bachan coming toward him.
Bachan's hand grabbed Richardson's wrist. That made
two.

Leverett was next, followed by Martinez. Then, in
rapid order, came John Corathers, Bill Wilson and Joe
Moore. That left one—Tom Delaney. Richardson felt a
light tap on his back. He shook his hand gently and Bachan
let go. Delaney moved in and grabbed Richardson and
Bachan. The star was complete. There were grins around
the circle as the men fell for another 15 seconds, then
broke apart. On by one their parachutes opened. Practice
was over for the day.

100 PERCENT SAFETY

A handful of Golden Knights have been injured in shows. More have been hurt in practice. "We still have the best record for safety of any sport parachute team," Sergeant Horn said. "Think of it. Seventy or more shows a year with at least four jumps per show, ever since 1959."

"We don't back out often, either," Richardson added, "If the wind is too strong (20 miles per hour or more), we may not jump. If the clouds are too low, the same.

"There's no problem in jumping in high winds. The problem is landing. The parachutes we use have a forward speed of about 22 miles per hour. We can use that speed to compensate for the wind. But when we touch the ground is when the fun begins.

Richardson explained that the wind will grab a parachute and drag the jumper across the ground if he isn't careful. "That's how bones get broken," he added. "Members of the team have had a number of cuts, bruises, and broken bones over the years."

Long before they make a demonstration jump, the Golden Knights look over their drop zone. One or two members check the area for buildings, trees, and power lines. They tell the rest of the team what they have found.

"Most of our jumps are at airports," another Golden Knight said. "Most airports are no problems. They've got wide open spaces. But we can jump almost anywhere. The closer we have to come to trees, power lines, or buildings, the more careful we have to be."

The Golden Knights seldom land anywhere but on target. Every once in a while, however, the target is on the water. They add an inflatable lifejacket to their jump gear.

"I don't mind the water jumps," one Knight said. "Sure, you get wet. But landing in the water is much softer than landing on the ground."

"The one landing area that scares me is trees," said another. "I went into some trees once and my parachute got hung up right at the top. I only had to drop eight to ten feet to the ground. It took two hours, though, to get the parachute out of the tree."

"In one demonstration, the wind started blowing harder after we took off," another recalled. "I was jumping with an old round parachute. I tried to fight the wind but it didn't work. It blew me over some buildings. I was lucky and landed on top of one of them. I got out of my harness just as the chute blew into some power lines."

The memory of one tragedy haunts the Golden Knights. Eleven jumpers and a flight crew of three crashed in one of their aircraft in 1973. All were killed.

"That was one of the worst times I can remember," said a Golden Knight. "The plane had just taken off from Fort Bragg. It wasn't more that 50 to 70 miles from home when it went down.

"The news came in little by little. It took several hours before we knew what had happened. It was hard to take. I knew all of the guys who were killed. It was like losing family.

"We had a memorial service here at Fort Bragg, but most of the men were buried in their home towns. When we went back to doing shows, we weren't as good as we had been. It took several months before we got back into top form.

"The fall of 1973, we had one of the largest turnouts when we called for new members. Rebuilding the team after something like that was very hard, but we did it."

There were hundreds of rumors after the crash. Some said the pilot of the aircraft had told the jumpers to bail out. A later investigation showed that all 14 men had gone down with the plane, which apparently had engine trouble.

"There was a copy of the report in the office," said the Golden Knight. "I could have read it, but I didn't want to."

The crash was the only one in history that took the lives of an entire military performing team. It did not take place during a show. The team was on its way to a show site at the time.

JUMPING FOR GLORY

While the Golden Knights' Black and Gold teams jump for entertainment, their competition team jumps for awards.

Parachute competition is international. At least one Golden Knight has been a member of the United States team every year since 1960. Three of them have been international champions. They were James Arender (who won twice) in 1960 and 1962, Richard Fortenberry in 1964, and Clayton Schoelpple in 1972.

"There are ten different parachuting accuracy records," a Golden Knight said. "We hold eight of them. And in the 1975 national championships, we set a new accuracy record with ten perfect landings out of ten."

Each year, the competition changes. In even-numbered years, jumpers compete in style and accuracy. In odd-numbered years, they compete in "relative work," a team event.

"Style and accuracy competition may be a little easier. The men are judged on how they handle themselves in free-fall, and how they handle their parachutes. For accuracy, they try to hit a 10-centimeter disc in the drop zone," a Golden Knight explained.

"In 1976, we formed our first relative work team. We hadn't had one before. Relative work is more difficult. It involves total body control when you're free-falling. The judges watch through powerful telescopes and give grades. It's a little like springboard diving, I guess."

The big world parachuting event is called *Counseil International du Sport Militaire.* That's French.

"Teams come from behind the Iron Curtain, South America, Asia, and Europe to the Internationals," a Golden Knight said. "It was really an honor in 1973 and 1974. We—the United States, that is—won over-all honors in both meets. There was a conflict in dates in 1975. The United States didn't compete."

Sergeant Brake led the 1976 Golden Knights competition team into the nationals at Tallaquah, Oklahoma. From hundreds of jumpers, only ten—five men and five women—were to be chosen for the international team.

"We've had men in the top ten every year since we started competing," a Knight said. "We've won first in the over-all event in 1960, 61, 62, 63, 65, 70, 71, 73 and 74. Our best man has done no worse than second in any other year.

"Our record in national and international competition is probably the best of any team in the world," he added.

"We're hoping to change the rules for our competition team," Richardson commented. "In most countries, the military jumpers stay on their teams for years and years. A Golden Knight can only stay three years. We hope our guys will be given longer terms so the United States can have the best people possible."

"It makes me proud to belong to the competition team," a Knight said. "I haven't made the United States team yet but I will."

"The Golden Knights are supposed to represent the best of the United States army. I'm proud of that too. I hope we can bring more people into the Army with the work we do. And I hope that in watching us, the people of this country will be as proud of their Army as we are."

About the Author:

Peter B. Mohn published his first children's book in 1975. He still hasn't gotten over it. The **Golden Knights** is his 14th book. A native of Minneapolis, he now lives in a small town in Minnesota. He is a lover of sailing and outdoor sports. Peter has spent hundreds of hours researching the Golden Knights' air shows at their training at Fort Bragg, N.C.

INDEX

accidents, 40-43
accuracy (jumps), 44
air shows, 3-20
Arender, James, 44
Bachan, Mike Sgt., 14, 33, 39
barnstormers, 31
baton pass jump, 9-11
Black team, 32, 34, 44
Blue Angels, 16
Bordeleau, Bill Sgt., 5, 18
Brake, Sergeant, 46
Broadwich, Tiny, 31
Caribou (aircraft), 3-17
competition team, 30, 32, 34, 44-47
Corathers, John Sgt., 8-11, 39
Counseil International de Sport Militaire, 46
cutaway jump, 12-13, 14-15
"dead center" marks, 30
Delaney, Tom Sgt. 16, 39
demonstration teams, 32
diagram (landings), 22
Dillon, Al Sgt., 16
drop zone, 33-40
Dupuis, Roger Sgt., 14
"flag jump," 3-7
formation flight, 16, 36-37
Fort Benning, Ga., 24
Fort Bragg, N.C., 28, 32
Fortenberry, Richard, 44
free falls, 4-5, 9, 11, 12, 35
Golden Knight volunteers, 28-31
Gold team, 32, 44
Green Berets, 27
HALO school, 25
high altitude jumps, 27
honorary Golden Knights, 31
Horn, Glen Sgt., 28, 30, 32
"hot" (jump run), 35
international competitions, 44-47
jumps, types of, 3-17

jumpmaster, 27
jump school, 24-27
Leverett, Guy Sgt., 3-7, 39
malfunctions, parachute, 23
Martinez, Sergeant, 7, 39
McNeeley, Tim Sgt., 12-13
Moore, Joe Sgt., 16, 36, 39
packing up (parachutes), 17-20
parachute competitions, 44-47
parachute loft, 33
Para-Commander, 36
paratrooper training, 24-28, 32-40
physical training, 24, 32-40
practice (Golden Knights), 32-40
public relations, 22-23
Red Devils, 3, 5, 7
"relative" work, 44
reserve chutes, 15-19
reunion, 30-31
Richardson, Al Sgt., 3, 8, 16, 18, 34-39, 47
safety precautions, 40-43
Schoelpple, Clayton, 44
"slot" position, 16, 37
Special Forces, 27
speed in flight, 19
starburst, 37
star jump, 38-39
"static line" jumps, 26-27
Strato-Cloud parachute, 36
"streamer" chute, 12, 14
style (jumps), 44
team members, 33
tower jumps, 26
training for Golden Knights, 28-31, 32-40
trees, (danger of), 42
United States team (international), 44-47
water jumps, 42
Wilson, William Sgt., 8-11, 39
wind, effects of, 40-41
wingmen, 37
wind sock, 34